THE CUP AND SAUCER TREE

Memoirs of a Country Boy in Peace and War

By

A R LEWIS

Date of Publication:
December 1999

Published by:
Arcona

Printed by:
ProPrint
Riverside Cottage
Great North Road
Stibbington
Peterborough PE8 6LR

ISBN:0 9537576 0 9

THE CUP AND SAUCER TREE

CONTENTS:

PART ONE: CHILDHOOD

PART TWO: WAR

PART TWO CONTINUED

ACKNOWLEDGEMENTS

Acknowledgements are due to the following organisations and individuals for their invaluable help in the preparation of the manuscript. Newtown Library, Oswestry Library, North Shropshire College, The Writing Modern Poetry Group, Elaine Jones for the typing of the manuscript, Gwen Lewis, and all those kind enough to read preparatory drafts and to encourage me in the writing of this book.

Acknowledgements are also due to the undermentioned publishers:
Staple
Byword/United Press
Poetry Now
I D Books
Oswestry and Border Counties Advertizer
Powys County Times and Express
Daily Post, Liverpool

FOR MY WIFE
GWEN

PROLOGUE

Insects humming to green sun-speckled leaves,
Rays of bright sunshine dancing with flitting shadows,
All tuned to the touch of the summer breeze.
That's how it was and has always been.
And will remain. Secured in my mind.

As a young boy I gazed up at your beauty,
Admiring the curve of your saucer shape.
I stretched, jumping to view your cup,
Longing to climb you to taste your splendour,
Knowing that now we were bonded together.

When at last I climbed into your world,
I knew I was safe, nothing could harm me:
Your embrace, my own secret sanctuary.
Always when pain or danger threatened,
My mind would race to be safe in your cup.

Broken bones, Hospital spells, Schoolmasters' canes,
All failed to inflict any pain.
Hardship and danger, from Dunkirk to the Rhine,
All were as nothing and easy to bear:
You came to my aid, you never failed me.

When, as a boy, I lay down in your cup
To dream and plan my life-adventure -
I knew that you would always be there
To shelter and guide me wherever we went.
My Haven - My Harbour - In the tempest of life.

PART ONE

THE CUP AND SAUCER TREE
CHILDHOOD

1 THE CUP AND SAUCER TREE

For more than seventy years, I have kept secret my faith in that beautiful tree. And in all that time it has never failed me.

In times of great stress, and sometimes great danger, I simply climb up into its branches, letting my mind absorb its magic and I know I am safe in its embrace.

As a small boy, looking up into its thickly woven branches, I realised that in some way my life, and the tree would be bonded together. It was our destiny!

Standing up from the hedgerow, the round smooth trunk held up the saucer-shaped base, with its closely-knit, almost impenetrable branches. This in turn held the full shape of the cup, creating a perfect cup and saucer image in a living, breathing, natural tree.

How I longed to climb into its centre. I knew when that was achieved, I would be in my own private castle - my tower - my refuge - my place of sanctuary, where nothing could cause me harm. A green haven of peace.

It would be my secret, kept hidden away in my mind. My world, shared only with nature, perhaps a nesting finch or thrush. We would be safe, encompassed in green caressing leaves. Secure like a child in its mother's embrace.

Despite all set backs - a period in hospital, an arm broken on two occasions - I never lost that burning desire. One day soon I would fulfil that dream.

Even before that great day, the tree dominated my thoughts. At four years old, I sat in bed in the old TB Hospital at Gobowen, out on the verandah of the open ended wards, snowflakes blowing in on the foot of my bed. I was oblivious to icy winter winds, fits of coughing, horrible medicines, cold and huge spoonfuls of cod liver oil. I just thought and dreamed of my beautiful tree. Knowing that I would recover, be reunited with that secret world.

Eventually, the time came. I knew that my moment of glory was to hand. The tree would be climbed that weekend, or at least by the following Bank Holiday Monday.

I remember the intense excitement, the anticipation of what was to come. Chores were carried out quickly and cheerfully. My mother became suspicious; I heard her remark 'That little devil is up to something.'

Oh I was, and a lot higher up than she thought.

My first attempt, despite all the planning, was a complete failure. It became apparent that during the time that I waited to grow strong enough, I had also grown quite considerably. Alternative routes to the summit had to be explored.

Eventually, the first part was achieved. I was in the saucer. Even that brought great delight and spurred me on to greater efforts.

Squirming and wriggling my way up into the cup, I lay there, my mind and body overcome with emotion.

Everything I had dreamed of was at last true. The sense of achievement and, above all, a feeling of complete safety. I was alone, as one with this living and breathing tree, almost a part of nature itself. Nothing could possibly harm me.

After all this time, scraped knees, scratched hands and a torn jersey seem such a small price to have paid for such high rewards.

2 GOBOWEN 1927

Snow flakes fell on the foot of the bed.
The children lay still, wide eyed, black rimmed,
Coughing, crying, young faces contorted in fright.
The cold so intense many wet the bed.

Nurses rushed round in their coats and scarves,
Serving out diets of boiled fish, potatoes in skins.
Coaxing and scolding, ensuring no one starved,
Then the big spoon, it's cod liver oil overflowing.

The generators constant with their gentle humming.
The clanging of metal jugs and bowls in the morning.
Then the change in the storm that came in the night,
With the rain and the hail on tin roofs drumming.

Little eyes, from troubled minds, peeped out;
For the wards had no walls to the sides and the front.
What were they all thinking? Surely not of heaven!
Fresh air was the cure for T B in 1927.

3 IN THE BEGINNING

The image of the Cup and Saucer tree dominated my early childhood.

I was born in the village of Caersws in the county of Montgomeryshire on the 1st December 1919. My home was a small old black and white cottage in Bridge Street and is still lived in today. I remember little of this cottage.

My earliest memories are of living in another black and white cottage on the estate of that great man, Lord Davis of Llandinam. This was a tied cottage. My father and my uncle worked on the estate. The cottages were called Waterlow Cottages, they were in fact two semi-detached houses. Our neighbour also worked on the estate, looking after all the beautiful Shire horses. My memories of him are always pleasurable ones. He was usually dressed in tweed jacket, breeches and leggings, and boots all shining and polished. His children all went to Llandinam School. We went to Caersws Council School.

This was a most pleasant place to grow up in. One could wander at will over fields and woods and, on occasions, play on the banks of the River Severn. On summer evenings one could watch the big fish jumping clear of the water, to land back with a resounding splash. Then, if lucky, see otters at play, ducking and diving, as they enjoyed each other.

Gypsies camped in the lane behind the house, their horses and coloured caravans forming a peaceful scene. Their dogs were always alert and let their owners know as soon as a stranger approached.

Up on the hills a herd of Welsh mountain ponies trotting on the horizon, manes flowing, led by the herd stallion. Could these be the same ones, observed a few days later, being herded down the road, eyes flaring, mouths frothing, on their way to the stock pen at the station? Then on to spend their lives in complete darkness in the mines of South Wales?

Across the road, enclosed in two paddocks by ten foot high wooden fencing, the two enormous Shire Stallions, each in his own compound, lazily swished their tails and twitched their muscles to dislodge the troublesome flies which always seemed to be in attendance.

Swifts, Swallows or House Martins swooped in and out of the open doors of the stable in the corner. Another place of secrecy to be explored, where one could perhaps see the birds at close quarters.

All this planning and pleasure of secret enjoyment had to be shared with that other necessity for children - school. But even that was disrupted for a short time, by an accident which later turned into a calamity. Falling off a box not more than a foot high, resulted in a broken arm.

This required a visit to the Doctor, who at once grabbed my arm, pulled and stretched it, at the same time turning it, to allow the bones to grate back into place. The spasm of excruciating pain this caused called for quick action - that is to say a swift kick where it hurt most, resulting in more pain. Finally the arm was splinted up, bandaged and held firmly in a sling, not to be used for at least six weeks. A dismal situation, no 'Cup and Saucer' climbing.

After about five weeks things seemed to be getting back to normal. If the tree was impossible, then perhaps the stable would be worth a try. A quick glance showed the stallion quietly grazing at the far end of the paddock, an ungainly hop over the stile, and I was in the stable, even before the house martins realised it. Once inside, the dark interior seemed unsafe, but a one armed climb into the manger, and then a final heave up into the hay rack above, which was half full of old hay, providing a safe comfortable observation post.

The half cup shapes of the mud nests, sticking to the beams and rafters seemed to be empty. A flash of blue and white and the parent bird was in, clinging to the nest edge now full of gaping mouths. She popped something into a mouth, picked something up in her beak, then out through the door in another flash of colour. This really was fast food service.

4 THE SHIRE STALLION

Where are you now, my gentlest Giant?
Friend of my childhood, and my brave Standard Bearer.
I remember so well the battles we fought -
Waterloo, Inkerman, Ladysmith.

We were so brave, you carried me, reins held taut:
The Red Dragon of Wales, our Standard proclaiming.
Those battles we fought in times without number,
Often at night, just before sleep.

Our friendship and trust will always endure,
Even when you left me with all that pain.
You were sold on, just like a slave,
Nothing is left, we must be courageous.

Where are you now my big gentle Shire?
In fields of lush grass painted in daisies,
A cool stream's trickling music,
Its clear fresh water to sip when you thirst.
I do so hope that such is your rest.

5 THE DEEP BLACK SHADOW

The doorway filled with a deep black shadow, and the great figure of the huge grey stallion entered the small stable, head held high, nostrils flared, sniffing the air, seeking out whatever had invaded his space.

In the hayrack above the manger the small boy drew back in fear as the huge animal ambled up, sniffing and snorting. The boy almost dropped the half eaten apple he had been enjoying, then in a quavering voice, tried to soothe the animal, offering his apple in reward. The huge head dropped slightly and leaned forward and sniffed the offering, then the great mouth opened revealing two sets of enormous teeth, the grey lips quivered and, with the utmost care, the apple was taken so gently the shaking hand scarcely felt it go.

Nodding his head and smacking his lips the big gentle animal seemed to be saying 'Thanks little one, I enjoyed that treat.'

He took out the rest of his lunch; cheese sandwich and a Welsh cake or two, all were shared and eaten with such gentle manners that the boy lost all his nervousness and tickled the ears of his newly found friend. The boy chatted away and the horse swished his tail, occasionally nodding his head as though after profound thought he agreed with his young friend. Then planting his feet squarely, he closed his eyes and went to sleep, showing implicit trust and happy to share his stable.

The boy gazed at the beautiful animal and marvelled at the power of that neck and shoulders, the strength and grace of this gentle and graceful creature would remain in his memory for life.

A bond had been forged between the two and remained so for two summers and then sadly they parted company.

It was the custom in those days to take the animals in for the winter months and let them out again in late spring. In the case of the stallions, they were taken in to be cosseted and pampered, and then taken out on their travels to visit all their mares in the surrounding area. This meant a lot of washing and brushing, plaiting of tails and mane, all the decorations polished and shining, the great feet oiled and cleaned, bridle and back pad polished and reflecting all their surroundings. The handler too looking the part, jacket and breeches all clean and pressed, his boots and his leggings shining like cats eyes.

The boy was so proud, this magnificent powerful God of Nature was his friend and treated him as gently, as a mother does her baby.

Then, of course, after three full seasons he had to be sold, the owner had to prevent in-breeding amongst his charges, passed on to pastures new. The boy understood this, but that next summer was to be one that always had something missing and the boy often murmured under his breath 'Where are you now, my gentlest Giant? Think of me sometimes, I know I do you. As you roam, may it be in long green grass, in fields of buttercups and daisies, with a stream to stand in on hot summer days and quench your thirst at will. You were my first really true friend.'

6 THE HIDDEN BOY

School was enjoyed especially football and all sports. The one fly in the ointment was music lessons. Singing caused me more heartache than everything else combined. Totally tone deaf, unable even to harmonise, always the inevitable 'You lad, you, you,. and you. I can do nothing for you, out into the yard, pick up all the rubbish, then weed the flower beds!' Four young boys out in the yard, undecided whether to be pleased to be free, or sad because they had no singing voice. I don't know about the other boys, but even to this day I cannot open my mouth to sing in Chapel or anywhere else. I would give my right arm to be able to sing.

Always a short discussion. 'You lads can do what you like, I'm off.' This seemed to be my reaction, snatching up my school satchel, ducking under the window, across the playground, over the waste tip, jump to the top of the wall, over and away. A two mile run, then up into the Cup and Saucer tree, free as the wind, safe, and completely happy.

Few cars passed along that road in the late 1920s. Occasionally one would stop to admire my beautiful tree, unaware that a young boy was watching their every move. Sometimes a camera would be produced, and after a great deal of looking at various angles, a picture would be taken. I often wondered what those avid photographers would make of the small face grimacing at them, or the pair of rather large feet, encased in white plimsolls, sticking up on the rim of the cup, should the negative ever reveal the hidden boy.

7 LEAVING THE CUP AND SAUCER TREE

In the middle of all this enjoyable childhood, sudden disaster. My father lost his job on the estate and of course, no job, no house. A move followed and, although it was only about four miles to the adjoining village of Trefeglwys, it seemed another world. The house itself was a station house, 'Pwllglas Station', about a mile out of the village The railway line ran in front of the house. There was a big yard, a railway siding with trucks and wagons, and as there were only two trains a week, there were lots of places to explore in safety.

Monday morning in the new school brought the first shock. The children naturally all spoke Welsh, but when they realised that we only spoke English they did their best to involve us, but inevitably in the excitement of the playground they would revert to their first language. I was Welsh and very proud of being so. Why on earth was I not taught Welsh in school? The old prejudices of past ages lingered on, one village school disregarded the Welsh language, another, just four miles away, was strongly in favour.

The children, the local farmers and the people I came into contact with were perfectly friendly. However there was one difficulty - the Headmaster, who resented me, decided that I was a corrupting influence on his school and caned me whenever he could find the slightest fault. Not just caning; he would punch, slap and shake, muttering in Welsh, red in the face, completely losing his temper. It was then that I learned how to use the 'Cup and Saucer' safety area. In my mind I would climb the tree, then absolute peace, blotting out all pain, untouchable, look the bigot straight in the eye, and dare him to do his worst. He would never make me cry. I was safe. Thus the complete trust in the tree was established, and would be used constantly in War, and peace.

The pity of all this was the fact that I desperately wanted to learn to speak my native tongue. He simply beat it all out of me! Such a shame, especially as he had a very pretty daughter attending the school. I would have been very pleased to have been in her circle of friends.

Fortunately this episode did not last long. The unhappiness was noticed, and a return to my village of Caersws, and my old school reattended.

Although no longer living near the 'Cup and Saucer', it was easy to jog the couple of miles, climb the tree, and spend some hours of complete bliss, marred only by the absence of that great gentle giant the stallion, sold on to pastures new.

8 THE TREE REVISITED

The last year or so of my schooldays slipped by so quickly. One or two episodes still remain as sharp as ever in my memory.

Summer time lunch breaks, and a mad dash up past the station, into the fields to Carno Brook, a tributary to the River Severn. 'Last one in is a sissy.' Clothes flung in a heap on the bank. Splashing and swimming in the cool clear water. Occasionally someone would, in haste, and excitement, jump in with his socks still on, or even worse, his pants.

Although the river played a large part in our lives and gave great enjoyment, it also sometimes caused great concern. I remember two such occasions.

Near the bridge on Trefeglwys Road, a family lived in a red brick house, built in the small triangle of land between the railway bridge (no longer existing) and the road bridge. This house had a small blue plaque, stating that the Welsh poet, Caradoc Hughes, had once lived there. The water supply was by means of a large pipe which ran past the house and discharged into the river. Water was collected by means of leaning over the bank, and allowing a bucket to be filled from the discharging pipe, a hazardous method even in fine weather.

One lunch time a gang of boys, of which I was a member, was standing on the road bridge, trying to assess the river which was in full flood, and gauge how soon it would be before it broke over its banks, causing a flood, and our quick exit from school. We always got sent home when floods were threatened.

Suddenly there was a terrible screaming, and we could see someone being swept away down river, shouting and waving her arms. All we could do was race back to the station and raise the alarm. The poor lady was found the next day entangled with the barb wire, underneath the Severn Bridge. She had met her death by trying to catch a bucketful of water from the pipe. This was also in full spate, and the force of the water hitting the bucket dragged her into the river. It was weeks before any of us could stand on the bridge and look into the river.

One other incident also had a very lasting effect on the boys of the school. In the same spot, just near the railway bridge where the pipe discharged. It was a glorious sunny day, the usual gang of boys was on the river bank, looking into what was in fact a whirlpool. In the clear water you could see the water going round and round, a stick thrown in would follow the flow, sinking down, and then slowly swirling back up again.

Suddenly one of the boys slipped in and was carried round and down. His twin brother jumped in to try and save him. Neither could swim. One lad raced off to get help from the station yard. The rest of us watched in horror as both boys were swirled round and down, and then we could plainly see them crawling up the gravel slope of the bank, where we quickly grabbed them, coughing and spluttering, but otherwise apparently none the worse for their experience. A very quiet group of boys received a roasting from the two men who had raced up from their workplace, no doubt expecting to have to reclaim two drowned boys from the well known whirlpool.

The boys of the school had their own fighting arena, this was the square public weigh-bridge, which was let into the road near the station. The metal square formed a perfect arena, and the press of children round the edge ensured the best possible enclosure. Any disagreement in the school resulted in the challenge 'see you on the weigh-bridge after school!' If the challenge was taken up, the news would go round the school like wild fire, and everyone rushed to get a first class viewing spot. Many reputations were made and broken on that weight-bridge. My reputation was never challenged, after all, I was at least six inches taller and much heavier than my contemporaries.

A move to the County School at Newtown proved to be impossible and I would have to leave school at 14 years of age. Therefore, an alternative plan for my education had to be worked out. Acting on the advice of an old retired policeman, my future life was mapped out. That is to say wait until I was 18, then join the Guards, further my education, leave after three or four years. Join the Police Force. Retire after the stipulated 25 years on a good pension, and still a comparatively young man.

9 PIT PONIES AND FIREFLIES

I crept out of bed quietly, when the house was asleep,
Then out the back door, and up into my tree.
This was the way to watch the fireflies play.
I settled down to creep into the lives of those not sleeping.
The screech of a vixen, like a maiden in terror,
Such a strange way to summon a lover,
But it must be the strongest to make her a mother.

It was then that I saw them, on the brow of the hill,
Dark shapes of such beauty, in black silhouette;
The proud black stallion, long main flowing,
His brood behind him, following.
Maybe a hundred horses, the young and the old,
So wild, so free, going to rest in some secret place.
The scene so intense, the fireflies forgotten,
They could not match the spectacular sight.
Of so many horses tossing their heads in the night.

I dawdled to school one morning later, still thinking,
And scheming how to observe without causing fright,
Those graceful, coal black creatures I saw.
Then I heard shouting and cracking of whips,
And the sound of unshod hoofs, on hard tarmac tapping.
Then, they came into sight and in place of their leader
Rode a man on a horse demanding they follow,
With two more behind, whistling and shouting,
Lashing their whips from left and to right.
Eyes glaring, nostrils flaring, open mouths frothing,
Bodies all flecked with their sweat and their spittle.
I drew back in horror as they passed in terrified flight,
Could these be the beautiful creatures I had seen in the night?

Rounded up, herded into pens, they waited
Listening to the clank of shunted cattle trunks.
The weaker horses stood, heads bowed in defeat,
But a few still raised their's high to neigh defiance.
All longed for the freedom of Firefly hill,
But they were now part of a human cash crop.
I stayed with them for all of that morning -
Schoolboys are right to rebel when they are in grief:
For those sweet creatures were doomed, some to go blind
Deep in the earth where man and horse mined.

That night as I watched the fireflies flitted;
They did not excite me, I wanted to see
That proud black stallion with all that remained
Of his large family, still running wild and always free.
I never saw him again, but I heard him that night,
His snorting and stamping and anxious whinnies.
His neighing drifted down on the darkness it stirred,
As he searched and pleaded in vain for the rest of the herd.

Now as I grow older, I still think of them,
Deep under ground in the stale air and dust.
Do they think of their sweet life on the hill?
When they see lights on human heads nodding,
As they toil together, the fireflies mocking,
And is that the sound of a vixen's screech?
Or the scream of a human under a rock fall?
There are no winners, just losers in this underground hell,
Where day means night and all day all night.
Does some kind collier with work worn hands
Gently wash off the dust and the grime
To let them breathe freer and see just a bit?
Think kindly of me as you leave me behind,
For I cannot help you, except in my mind.

10. THE RIVER

You lazily wander, through pastures green,
Curling your way as you flow to the sea.

Sand Martins, Kingfishers, live in your banks.
Tail-swishing cattle, stand cooling their flanks.

The sunshine reflecting the Golden Gorse
In shallows you gurgle your baby talk;

Why do you rush to be lost in the sea?
Linger a little, the sights to enjoy.

And feel the beauty your presence inspires.
Talk to the rainbow trout, his beauty admire

As he grows fatter on the food you provide,
Why do you rush to meet up with the tide?

In your deep pools, the predatory pike prowls,
Greedily snapping up any smaller souls,

He doesn't rush off to be part of the sea.

11. WHERE DO WILD DUCKS NEST?

The three young boys scoured the banks of the river, risking a soaking, clambering out over the water on over-hanging trees, wading back to check possible nesting sites. They were in search of a wild duck's nest. This was the one that eluded them all spring. All other water birds like the moor hen had been fairly easy to see, sitting on their nests, nervously watching, ready to take off should danger threaten.

They were in no danger from the boys, whose desire was simply to find the nests and note their existence, and observe them without disturbance.

A wild duck was a water bird, so where would it nest except on the water? It seemed logical to the boys, who talked and argued about it continuously.

It was during one of these arguments, whilst sitting on the river bank enjoying the shade of an Alder tree, that the boys were suddenly shocked to hear a voice saying 'And what are you young shavers up to?' It was old Mr Jones, the river bailiff. Boys usually made a hasty retreat when approached by any form of authority. This time, however, they stood their ground, explained their problem and, knowing that he had a great knowledge of the river bank, asked him for the solution. After a good deal of questioning and having to prove that the nests they found were completely safe, the bailiff startled the boys by telling them that the wild duck more often than not nested in hollow trees, twenty feet or so off the ground. The boys were so surprised by this that they began to think that they were being hood-winked. Surely, they argued, ducks were water birds. The kindly old bailiff simply said 'Follow me and keep quiet.' A little way up river he stopped and pointed to an old tree about twenty yards from the river bank, some fifteen feet off the ground. A hollow, where a branch had broken off, could clearly be seen, and there peeping over the edge, the female duck.

The boys were so amazed at this revelation and so full of eager questions, that the old chap simply smiled, consulted his note book, pondered for a moment, then having made up his mind, told the boys that the duck would probably hatch her brood sometime between Friday and Monday the next weekend, and that the boys should mount a nest watch and try and see the vital hatching. This, he promised, would be a sight to remember all their lives. This should be for their eyes only, no spilling the beans, causing a crowd of horrible young idiots to disturb the peace.

The boys made for the river bank on the Friday, grabbing their tea and eating it on the run. They were relieved to see the bird still on its nest. Saturday passed slowly and eventually hunger made the three lads give up and seek sustenance. The duck was also getting restive, making clucking sounds. The lads decided to head back to the village, spend all their pocket money purchasing fish and chips, then return for a final evening watch.

Thus fortified, and feeling much more satisfied, they raced back to their watch duties. On nearing the nest they were alarmed to hear the agitated quacking of the female duck. She seemed to be greatly alarmed. The boys crept up, staring in wonderment. The duck had left the nest and was calling urgently to her brood, peeping down from their nest fifteen feet above. Then the miracle happened, the little bundles of brown and yellow simply jumped off the nest, landing with a soft plop, then waddled away to their mum, all twelve of them, straight onto the water swimming and feeding without a care in the world.

For a long time the boys argued and pondered at the wonders of nature. How did the tiny bundles of feathers jump unhesitating from their nest and into the water without a trace of fear? Truly nature is a miracle.

12. READING THE RIVER

Lulled to sleep by the pleasant murmur of the river as it prattled and chortled over the shallows, the two boys slept the sleep of the young.

Their makeshift camp, just an old scrap of tarpaulin held up by a stick at each corner, enabled them to look out in every direction, for it had no walls. Their imagination converted it into a ship at sea, an Indian tepee, or a soldier's bivouac on the North West Frontier. It had been their home for a week now, and was just far enough away from their real homes to be exciting, but near enough to dash home when the craving for food became too strong.

They practically lived in the river: a swim in the morning instead of a wash, a run along the bank to dry themselves. Then the fire lit, a hunk of bread toasted and burned almost black, dipped in the old frying pan to soak up some fat. Butter rations disappeared on the first day! Water boiled and poured over the dregs of last night's tea, no milk or sugar, the old enamel jug scalding hot. What a feast to start the day.

Towards afternoon the clouds up the valley appeared to be crowding in, black and threatening. Like true explorers, the weather was gravely discussed. 'Rain in the hills at the head of the valley, no worry to our camp.'

After a quick dash up to the village, fish and chip supper and a bottle of lemonade, they settled down for a long sleep, listening to the prattling of the river as it gurgled and murmured over the shallows. Surely no one could wish for a sweeter lullaby.

They woke at dawn to see the sun beginning to emerge behind the hills, but what was wrong? The two intrepid explorers both felt it - something had happened in the night. On going to the river for their usual swim-wash, it became obvious that there had been rain, a lot of rain, up in the hills. The river had risen in the night. Now it was about a foot deeper, the sound of it changed completely. Instead of the gentle lullaby sounds of the night before, it was now swishing along in a swift menacing manner and had taken on a darker, deeper colour. Too cold for a swim, a quick face splash would have to suffice. The two boys would always remember how to read the sounds of the river.

Years later, one of the boys, a soldier at war in Belgium, would have cause to bless that day he learned to read the sounds of a river. His Company, after a lot of fierce fighting, had managed to secure a bridge over a small river. Now they had to hold it secure to ensure a quick advance the following day. The river was too shallow for any danger from underwater frogmen to attempt an explosive attack. Awakening from an uneasy sleep, the soldier immediately sensed that something was wrong. And then it came to him. He was once more a lad camping by the river and that river had changed just as this one was doing now, and in a flash he realised the significance. The enemy had prepared a diversion somewhere up-stream, causing a two foot rise in depth, and still rising. There had been no rain. Obviously something was about to happen. Sure enough, a short patrol up-stream came upon an enemy contingent preparing for a frogman approach to blow up the bridge.

Reading the sounds of the river had truly paid off. The next day, the Brigade transport crossed the bridge without difficulty to relieve another part of the Belgian countryside.

13. FIRST KISS BY THE RIVER

The river in shallows murmured and chattered.
In deep pools, sighing, swishing and swirling.
The sun blazing down on great patches of gold,
The Gorse bushes popping, their seed pods exploding;
While the Broom gently swayed, wafting its perfume
On the delicate touch of the breeze from the River.

Nature itself could not have been kinder
That day, as we walked in its splendour.
We shyly held hands - it was our first meeting.
Then, we sat on the grass in quiet conversation.
Long pauses, deep sighs, then trickles of words,
Nervous laughs, like the sounds of the river
As it flowed past our feet.

We turned to each other with lips slightly pouting,
Both of us nervous of that very first kiss.
Our lips barely touched, like a butterfly flutter,
Or was it a puff from the wind on the river?
Your sweet tiny face seemed mounted in gold,
Eyes open wide and Kingfisher-blue.

New love, young love, needs time to mature,
But we drifted apart, then found love once again.
True love, mature love, but not with each other.
Yet still the Broom, its perfume heart stopping,
And the Golden Gorse goes on pleasing
Down by the river, for other loves walking,
Just as it did when we were so young.

14. PLAYING WITH FISH.

To play with fish? Well, it is possible:
So long as your hands are gentle, and patient.
He lies there quietly, tail slowly waving,
Then a quick pounce, at some morsel he fancies.
Now lay flat on your stomach, hands outstretched,
Next work one hand slowly, up behind him,
The other hand moves to reach out in front,
Then drop in a worm without making a splash,
And when he dives forward to grab at his catch,
Just move your hand up from whence he started,
Now he'll float back to his favourite spot.
This time it's your hand on which he settles,
Just let him get used to its different feel,
Then slowly allow your fingers to tremble,
Tickling his tummy, and just like a puppy,
He will wriggle and squirm, asking for more.
You can now try a worm held between fingers,
Be patient and wait till he spots it.
Then he'll move forward and eat from your hand;
And that's when you say - 'Yes, play, play,
I play with the fish in the river.'

15. JUVENILE POACHERS

The Severn curled its lazy way through fields of daisies and buttercups, its banks alternating from steep sides to gravel shores. From deep forbidding pools to murmuring, bubbling shallows. Where cows stood knee deep, cud chewing, tails swishing to dislodge troublesome flies. The sun blazing down from the clear blue sky, where small fluffy clouds looked down and seemed to smile their approval.

Two boys walked slowly along the banks, talking quietly, not to disturb the wildlife around them, but in earnest, serious conversation, each making profound statements as only twelve year olds can. They carried a thin but strong hazel stick, looking like undersized javelin throwers on their way to some Olympian contest. Every few minutes they felt in their pockets to reassure themselves that the thin strand of wire, carefully unravelled from the wire rabbit snare they had begged from their elders, was now neatly coiled and safe, ready for use.

Their sharp eyes scanned the water. Having long since perfected the knack of looking through the surface of the water to the bed of the river, this was an absolute necessity if they were to become successful in their devious pursuit.

Large tracts of the Severn were too wide, too deep, or too open to suite them. What they were looking for was a small tributary which would gurgle and trickle over rocks, where the brown trout loved to hide under cover in the shade. Some would lie on the pebbly stretches of shallow water, lazily dreaming in the sun-flecked stream, too full to even attempt to gobble up a passing insect. These were the fish the two lads had been seeking. Swiftly, surely, the thin brass wire would be secured to their sticks, the noose on the end tested and found to run true. A careful look up and down stream to make sure the water bailiff was not on patrol, then almost delirious with excitement and anticipation, their work would start. Each selecting a small stretch of water, creeping cautiously along, trying not to create a tall thin shadow, these fish would be used to seeing the shapes of sheep or cattle, but an upright human figure would be strange and suspicious. Selecting their fish, the stick would be gently lowered into the water a couple of yards upstream and allowed to float gently down toward the fish, the noose of the wire opened sufficiently to pass around its body, then once past its gills, a quick flip of the stick and a lovely fish would lie on the river bank glistening and gasping. A quick tap on its head made sure that the suffering was brief. It was possible to become so good at this type of poaching, that when the wire had encircled the fish it could be gently twisted, tickling the fish's belly, so that it wriggled with pleasure, making no attempt to escape.

When the open runs had been completed, a second and most exciting method would start. Quickly removing shoes and socks, and hiding them on the banks, the boys' sleeves rolled up, they started tickling the fish hidden under the rocks, sometimes lying flat on their stomachs, sometimes wading in the stream, hands feeling gently for the slippery touch of a fish, then slowly and cautiously exploring the length of it, a firm closing of the fingers behind the fins and, hey presto, another fish. The small or lesser fish would be quickly released, the larger fatter ones just as quickly dispatched. The boys were very river-wise and on catching a couple of fish, they used the long-established method of hanging them, well hidden, on a bit of string passed through the gills, in some overhanging branch of a tree. Should a poacher be caught by the bailiff, it was wise not to be in possession of ill-gotten gains.

16. THE WHITLOW

Looking down at his right index finger,
He saw the scar remained, as did that curved fingernail.
Not thought of for years, the memory was now vivid,
The whitlow, the pain, and the delirium,
And the heat of the bread poultice.

The old doctor flitting in and out of his dreams,
Muttering 'Not ripe, not ripe, I'll lance it tomorrow.'
From the pain and the poison, now light in the head,
He lay there, half in - half out of his bed, in despair.

Into his mind, drifted thoughts of wild creatures.
What would they do? And then he knew.
The bandages removed, the gangrenous finger exposed,
The putrid green spreading up into his hand.
He bit through the yellow skin with his strong teeth.

The poison now released, dripped onto the floor.
Relief from the pain, he was exhausted,
But his brain was now clear.
He lay back on his pillow and started to rest.

Then in a week he was back, throwing stones in the River!

17. THE PARTY KISS

We walked slowly home from the party.
The sky clouded over, it started to rain.
Taking off my coat, we snuggled beneath it.
It was exciting - I pressed my lips on your freckled cheek.
'Now you will have to marry me,' I firmly said.
You chuckled and lisped
'Oh, you are thoppy, you know we are too young.'
Smiling and revealing your missing front teeth.
You were just six, and I was seven,
And for that passing moment, I was in Heaven.

18. PLAYGROUND ROMANCE

That day started so well as we talked in the playground, we were young and innocent and you smiled as you gave me your pen. 'You may borrow it for a while to improve your writing' at least that's what you said, or was it perhaps you knew that I could not afford to buy one for myself?

That was the nicest and most exciting thing that happened to me all that school term. You actually liked me enough to let me borrow that golden, green pen with its screw top, and which caused all the heartache. It had been screwed on too tightly, and clumsy oaf that I was, I twisted and turned it, and horror of horrors, the beautiful pen snapped and broke into two!

I skulked in the playground, afraid to confront you until, at last, I was forced into telling the awful truth. I will never forget the look on your face, as I showed you the broken pen and attempted to apologise. Your expression told me the dreadful truth. I had broken your trust. I ran off in despair, in case you said something, and discovered the tears in my eyes.

19. CLODDING

In the 1930s almost the only means of transport was the bicycle, everyone had one. A few older people rode their horses and it was still possible to see an old farmer leave the pub on a market day, climb into the saddle, fall asleep and allow his horse to take him home quite safely.

The village youths were very parochial and resented lads from nearby villages invading their territory, and stealing their girls. At dances and other functions, all would be strictly formal, and fraternisation would take place without any problems. It was only when an outsider was allowed to escort a young lady home that the trouble started. This often meant a mile or so walk; wheeling a bicycle with one hand and attempting to encircle the girl's waist with the other was extremely difficult. Occasionally, once clear of the actual village, the girl would allow herself the 'luxury' of having a ride on the crossbar of the lucky chap's bicycle. With a girl on your crossbar, her hair blowing in the wind, your face close to hers and both arms around her, many romances matured to lasting love.

Having escorted the young lady home and succeeded in obtaining a kiss and a cuddle, or quite often just a quick 'Goodnight', the return journey had to be faced, with the pretty sure knowledge that somewhere along the road the village lads would be waiting. Not to brutally attack you, but unseen behind the hedge, armed with clods of earth, and sometimes something more messy, just to give the young upstart a gentle warning. The only thing to do was to get up as much speed as possible, sail through the missiles, trusting that the lads were not from the village cricket team.

If the intruder had serious thoughts about his new girlfriend, then he would show his tormentors that he would continue, despite their rather pathetic warning. Switching off his cycle lights, and dodging through a convenient gate, waiting until his assailants had passed, he would cycle at just sufficient speed to overtake, pass them calling out 'Goodnight' and, if known, mention their names. Then, whistling and pretending he had not a care in the world, he cycled off home.
This was usually sufficient to proclaim that his intentions were honourable and that nothing was going to stop his future liaisons.

20. THE THRESHER'S LAMENT

Up the blutty ladder,
Start work on the Thresher.
My guts are all on fire.
Down the blutty ladder.
Crouch behind the shed.

Up the blutty ladder.
Started work once more.
Diawich! my old guts again.
Down the blutty ladder.
Crouch behind the shed!

Once more up the ladder,
And start up once again.
My gut still on fire.
Down the blutty ladder
Don't reach the shed.

I tell you, I tell you -up
And down the blutty ladder,
Down behind the shed!
There, I shit two farts,
And now, I fart one shit!

PART TWO

THE CUP AND SAUCER TREE WAR

1. THE GUARDS' DEPOT

The rhythmic thudding of Army boots,
The shouted commands in many voices,
Squads of recruits in red-faced concentration,
As they marched this way and that, then back again,
Saluting to each side, and then to the front;
So much to learn in so little time.

Dashing around from one place to the other:
Gym, Barrack Square, School Room, and Swimming Pool.
And always the threat of extra fatigues:
Spud-bashing, washing of dishes, cleaning toilets
All formed part of a Recruit's full day.
Then still to find time for cleaning his kit.

Drill - drill - then drill some more!
Then do it all again, this time with rifles.
Slope, salute, present arms, all done to numbers,
To get the rhythm right, so they said.
Sore feet, sore shoulders, fingers all numb,
God help the man who dropped his rifle.

N C O's, trying to out-shout each other,
'My squad is sharper, and smarter, than yours.
I might just kill the bastards to prove it!'
Physical fitness, the key to it all?
Although now soldiers, we had not fired a rifle,
Just cleaned and polished it, inside and out.

Button polish, boot polish, Blanco-white and khaki,
Toothpaste, soap, razor blades and flannel,
All to be purchased with a recruit's meagre pay
Leaving just enough for a cup of NAAFI tea.
Letters home and to friends got rarer and rarer,
Stamps cost money, and we all liked a smoke.

Then out of this chaos a Soldier emerged!
Not just a Soldier - A Guardsman, no less,
Now to be part of the Army Elite.
Trained to fight with rifle and bayonet,
To uphold and defend the honour of Wales:
'Hwy clod na hoed!' - Fame lasts longer than life.

2. ARMY ENLISTMENT

On the 1st December 1937, reaching the age of 18 years, I became old enough to join the Army to commence the second phase of my life's plan and start getting a better education.

The recruiting sergeant at Newtown, a fat jovial Sergeant, seemed eager to sign me up! A 6ft 2in youth, weighing about 15 stone would apparently be welcome into the Regiment of His Majesty's Welsh Guards. But first I had to produce two character references from people of some standing in the community.

The local doctor said he would be delighted to give me a reference and congratulated me on my initiative. (This was not the doctor of the broken arm incident.)

My second choice was the local School Master, even though the old head had left, and I did not know the new one. Full of confidence I made the request, politely explaining that my idea was to further my education and that this was the only way possible. I fully expected him to congratulate me, as the Doctor had done, but was completely taken aback to be told that I should be ashamed of myself. Did I not know that soldiers were scum? Drinking and fornicating wherever they went. They were the dregs of humanity. Stay put and get myself a farm job like others did! Another bigot! I thanked him politely and told him to keep his reference . . . . Who could have guessed that within two years he would be crossing the road, trying to shake my hand, gushing clap trap?

On being told of the School Master's reaction, the old retired policeman stepped in and gave me a glowing reference, complaining that I should have gone to him in the first place.

The recruiting Sergeant seemed pleased, filled in the forms, handed over the King's Shilling and the travel warrants for the Guard's Depot at Caterham. He also had another recruit, a young man from Berriew. We travelled down together.

The introduction to Army life was a little surprising. On ringing the bell on the main gates, a large man with three stripes on his arm, a green band round the peaked cap - which seemed to be balanced on the bridge of his nose - enquired, not unkindly, what we wanted. To join the Welsh Guards' we replied. 'Now are you sure you've come to the right place? You'd best try the similar pair of gates just a few hundred yards further down the road, if they won't have you there, then come back here.' The gates were duly inspected, the word 'Asylum' could plainly be seen. Even two country yokels like us got the message. We returned to the Sergeant (we later realised he was in the Irish Guards) who, beaming like a jovial Father Christmas, said 'Come in lads, if they won't have you the Welsh will. After all they have a damn sight more sense than most bloody Welshmen.' It seems that this was the standing joke with whichever regiment was on Guard Duty.

That first night was a sleepless one. The wretched clock on the big tower chimed every quarter hour, absolute torture. At 6 am the whole place came alive, bugles blowing, men shouting, bedlam' what had I committed myself to?

3. LEARNING TO BE A SOLDIER

The system of recruits' training in 1938 meant that individuals, on enlisting, had to wait until sufficient numbers arrived to form into a squad of about twenty. Then the training really got started.

The period of waiting was always referred to as being 'unsquadded'. When asked by an N C O or officer who you were, the expected reply would be 'Recruit Number . . ... ,' your name and 'unsquadded'. This term seemed to imply that, to be 'unsquadded', you were not just a nobody, but a non-person doomed to continuous fatigues of sweeping the roads, cleaning toilets, working in the cookhouse, until that day when you again became human, not much of a human, (but one at least 'squadded' and able to live again).

Then the training really commenced, every second of every day, from reveille to lights out accounted for. One simple mistake caused instant chaos. Each squad was assigned an instructor, a corporal or other N C O and a trained soldier, usually a Guardsman of many years service. The N C O's were always refereed to by rank and always in full, the brigade of Guards did not tolerate sloppy abbreviations like Corp or Serge!

Their duties were divided into two parts. All outside training, marching, arms drill, saluting, were the N C O's responsibility. All activities in the barrack room; cleaning of equipment, the barrack room itself, were the job of the trained soldier, plus the teaching of military history of the Welsh Guards. You were expected to know all the battle honours, the names of all the N C Os, Warrant Officers and Officers of the regiment, and all the medals won by them in action. This was quite a mammoth task in itself; plus all the drill movements, both with and without weapons, all the various parts of your rifle, all had to be absorbed. Even the method and drill of your walking out cane (all Guardsmen carried a swagger cane when in uniform and off duty), was quite an elaborate performance.

Thus from the first notes of reveille, it became all go, wash, shave, clean your barrack room, toilets, bathroom, fold bedclothes and set your kit out in the approved manner. Grab your food utensils, bolt your breakfast, clean everything used, and an extra polish for everything. Room inspection by the duty officer and heaven help any poor unfortunate who hadn't done absolutely everything correctly. Buttons polished, even the cleaning utensil spotless. One of the more difficult things was the folding of blankets, sheets and towels etc. These had to be folded so precisely, if they were an eighth of an inch out of square the whole lot would be tipped up into a heap, sometimes tossed out of the window, even when four or five storeys high. The worst part was that the whole squad could be punished for a misdemeanour of one of its members. Thus the incredible feeling of comradeship was installed right from the start; all for one, one for all, each helping the other. Any bits of clothing or equipment spoiled or lost had to be paid for out of the individual's pay.

The work schedule was exhausting. Drills of all descriptions, PT exercises, swimming, all timed to perfection, changing from one outfit to another counted in seconds. One almost ate to deadly precision.

Then every evening, two hours of sitting on beds, polishing and cleaning, always with special attention to boots. These big heavy boots, when new, were of thick leather, the surface all bubbly, like an elephant's hide. This had to be polished until it became smooth and pliable, like patent leather. There were several ways of getting this result, some were illegal, like heating the back of a spoon and burning them smooth. When smooth, a piece of bone (sheep's ribs were particularly good) dipped into polish, and vigorously applied in a smoothing motion' then after all that, the good old spit and polish.
All this was the responsibility of the trained solder, who oversaw everything, continuously barking out questions to everyone about the Regiment, its Battle Honours, Regimental Officers, history of the Brigade of guards, those honoured in battle, etc. Anyone failing to answer correctly was immediately punished by a period of floor polishing. This was done with a long handled polisher, an ingenious thing called a 'floor bumper', consisting of a heavy polishing block on a swivel, which allowed it to stay flat on the floor whilst being propelled backwards and forwards by the long handle. Needless to

say, the wooden floor, after years of polishing by this means, gleamed as though made of glass.

After three weeks of this it was considered that perhaps you were trained sufficiently to be let out one evening a week. You lined up to be inspected by the trained soldier, who meticulously measured everything, including the winding of the puttees so carefully wound round your legs. When he was satisfied, you strode down to the barrack gates, arms swinging, swagger cane correctly balanced, to be again inspected by the Sergeant of the Guard. He could be a member of any of the five Regiments of foot guards. You marched up, halted as smartly as you could, and then were often sent back to the end of the queue because he was not satisfied with some petty detail. Eventually you emerged to 'live it up' for a few hours in the flesh pots of Caterham. Caterham was a garrison town, living and breathing the Brigade of Guards, and many a Guardsman rookie regretted misbehaving in town.

4. JOINING THE REGIMENT

Finally, after fifteen weeks of training, our little squad of recruits was pronounced fit enough to join the Regiment, then in residence at Albuhera Barracks, Aldershot.

There we were fitted out with Busby, Red tunics, Greatcoats and white webbing, the traditional uniform of the Guards. The most difficult bit of new clothing was the traditional grey cape, which had to be folded in a particular way into a small rectangle to specific dimensions, strapped in white webbing and carried on your back just across the shoulder blades. Any officer ordering the capes to be worn in inclement weather was extremely unpopular, as it meant unrolling them. On return to barracks, hours of work returning them to their rectangular shape of approximately 14" by 6" by 2".

Three months later found the Regiment in Wellington Barracks, London, duties Guard Mounting, Buckingham Palace, St James' Palace and the Bank of England. All interesting but just a little boring after a time. These Guards were always referred to as Buck, Jimmies and Bank. The first two were 24 hour Guards. The Bank Guard was strictly just a Picket Guard, night duty only, and simply meant marching to and then disappearing into the bowels of the Bank of England, not experiencing natural light or air all night. One post was considered to be haunted. The stain on the ceiling was rumoured to be the blood of a Guardsman who had shot himself whilst on duty. This was the only Guard where live ammunition was issued.

'Buck' Guard was considered to be the best one. The sentries, pre-war, patrolled outside the gates and railings, and were in touch with the public. This led to some strange meetings. The worst nuisance was that of model girls, starlets, etc, with their photographers and agents trying to get a picture to enhance their clients' careers. I could never work out why a picture of a girl looking adoringly at a sentry, with Buckingham Palace as a background, was considered to be of an advantage. Sometimes a pretty girl would pop a note into the barrel of your rifle. Occasionally, so did strange old men. The pretty girls of course got a smile and a wink, the strange men got the shock of their lives: the sentry springing to attention, taking a sharp step forward, the big army boots crashing down on his toes.

Rumours of war were starting to circulate. Suddenly, War appeared inevitable, but the War Office seemed not to worry. The only activity of aggression was the filling of thousands of sand bags for the protection of Government buildings.

This pleasant posting was ended abruptly with the order to hand in all public duty uniforms and equipment, together with civilian clothes, and prepare to move out.

We were never told of our destination until we were safely installed on a troop ship, and on our way toGibraltar.

TROOPSHIP

Crowded below deck, like cattle in transit,
We sit at tables on long wooden benches,
Bent almost double avoiding the hammocks,
The air now foul from the sweat and smoke.
We take turns for short periods on deck;
Discomfort even before we sailed.
Travelling just as they did in Nelson's day.

Ill timed jokes about plates of fat bacon,
Nervous laughter to avoid being the first
To rush to the sides, or heads, whichever is nearest.
Then the gentle swaying as we sail away.
Two hours out and soldiers turn green,
As their stomachs are emptied again and again.
This torture to continue throughout the voyage.

The decks awash with sick and bile,
Despite the hosing down at least every hour.
This blasted old tub, rising and wallowing.
Why does it not sink? It would be kinder.
And sill the dreaded Bay of Biscay to come.
When will we be free to leave this hell?
Soon, at last, warm Mediterranean sunshine.

6. THE ROCK

Gibraltar was a completely new posting for a Guards Regiment. Our normal postings were London, Windsor, Aldershot, and the Middle East.

Not being a 'good sailor' meant that the sea voyage became sheer hell. Seasickness from almost the first day confined me to either the ship's rail or the heads. In a comparatively short time, it seemed to me that almost all the troops were in the same condition. Leaning over the rail, being sick, became a very hazardous business. It appeared, on occasions, to be raining vomit. Those on the lower decks risked having someone on the deck above vomit down the back of their neck. The top deck troops, running to be sick on the windward side, had their own vomit blown back in their faces.

Those few days in crowded, airless, stench laden troop ship was the worst experience of my entire life. The decks, despite being hosed down with water, were always slippery with bile and vomit.

I think the ship was H M S Shropshire, almost certainly well past its 'sell by date.'

When, finally, we reached Gibraltar, the feeling of relief was overwhelming. A picture of me on the quay tells its own story. If I hadn't my rifle to lean on, I would probably have fallen over. I was so weak from that ghastly sea sickness! Thank Goodness I didn't join the Navy.

Duties on the Rock were quite light and surroundings and weather very pleasant. Trips to Tangiers, an open city, were very welcome. It seemed strange to see German sailors and soldiers strolling around on shore visits just as we were.

The only arduous tasks were assisting the Royal Engineers to carve yet more tunnels, making the centre of the rock rather like a huge underground station, with its own railway. We had, of course, our designated points of action stations should war be declared. It was at one of these defence positions on a fine sunny day, dressed in full fighting kit, on the beach leaning against the sea wall, that the expected news came through. 'We are now at war with Germany.'

In those few weeks our 'active service' consisted of being ferried out to so called 'neutral ships' which the Navy had caught trying to slip through the blockade of the Straits. These ships were all shapes and sizes; filthy cargo vessels with sheep, goats, chickens, all live and living in the holds for the sustenance of the crew. The stench was horrific, anchored up alongside smart new combined cargo and passenger ships. On one occasion, at least, a pleasure steamer containing over five hundred passengers and crew.

One section of Guardsmen was allotted to each ship regardless of size, that is, five or six men and one NCO. The orders were always the same; prevent the ship escaping or scuttling itself, call the roll of all passengers and crew at least twice every day. It took the authorities about seven days to clear the ship. In the meantime the section had to carry out continuous guard duties which usually meant one man on the bridge, one in the engine room and one on patrol over the deck, on a two hour on duty, two hours eat and sleep basis. The NCO of course had no relief, just grab odd times of sleep when possible. A totally impossible job. Fortunately I had the Cup and Saucer Tree to help me through.

7. THE ARMY KNOWS BEST

Whilst stationed in Gibraltar, I decided that marching was not really the way my career in the Army should be directed. I would be much better off in the Motor Transport section - riding was preferable to walking.

One day a notice appeared stating that corporals were required for transfer to other duties, any one interested should apply. The duties were:

1. Regimental Police.
2. Battalion Cook.
3. Transport Company, to be in charge of six mules (part of the inventory of Gibraltar station).

Here was my chance. Had I not worked with horses in civilian life? Surely I would be selected, and once in Transport Company, I would always remain so. The mules would be my ticket to ride.

My platoon commander agreed to forward my application, and he would personally put in a good word on my behalf.

Eventually, decisions were made. I was ordered to appear before the adjutant to be informed of his decision. He complimented me on my application, and informed me that he thought I would make a very good Regimental Policeman! Start tomorrow!

Complaining to my platoon commander, and enquiring as to why everything went wrong, he simply said there had been a complaint! Who, I enquired had complained? His reply was surprising - 'the mules.'

The Army moves in mysterious ways. I, who knew about animals, became a policeman. The transport job went to someone who had spent all his youth working with his father in his transport cafe! The cook's job went to someone, who, in civilian life, was employed in security at Cardiff Docks!

8. LEAVING THE ROCK

By November 1939 we had become restless in the confined space of Gibraltar, then to everyone's delight the order came to pack up, get ready to sail, re-issue Khaki uniform; most of us never really felt at home in tropical kit, and were glad to be rid of it. The question everyone asked was, where next? England seemed on the cards, but no, docking in Marseilles, we had a train journey across France to join British Expeditionary Force, first duties defence of Arras and Lord Gort's HQ. Action at last.

Awareness of what was about to happen should have been clear when it was announced that a fully trained Regiment of Foot Guards had been sent to strengthen the B E F. Most of that Regiment had never seen a tank at close quarters, or had one day's training in mechanised warfare. We were however lucky to be equipped with the new Bren Guns, a reliable machine gun which we used throughout the War.

According to the men in bowler hats from the ministry, our most potent weapon would be the new B O Y E S anti-tank rifle, a five foot long cumbersome lump of steel so heavy it was almost impossible to carry. This weapon, its name taken from the initials of the manufacturers, was quickly discarded, and condemned to an ignominious demise.

There was a period of quiet, later to be called the phoney war, and a particularly cold winter. Defensive positions were so cold that the water in our bottles froze, roads were a sheet of ice, the ground so frozen it became impossible to dig more fortifications.

9. BLITZKRIEG

As the weather and year changed toward summer, all hell broke loose, 'Blitzkrieg', advance of German tanks so quick it seemed no-one knew where the next attack was coming from.

On patrol in the goods yard of the town of Arras an awful noise of screaming animals, led us towards a big building which had been a stable block. Inside the partly demolished building was a scene from hell. Shire horses were panicking, some dead, all terrified. I thought of the beautiful Shire stallion of my youth, and anger surged up. Soldiers were supposed to be shot at in war, but animals came into the same category as women and children. How could I help? It seemed impossible, but opening the big main door, all the uninjured horses were let out. A terrifying task, they galloped off up the railway line towards open country and, I hoped, freedom. The poor animals too injured to walk I shot and left there where they fell. This episode made me so angry. We were supposed to be fighting Germans and yet here was I shooting and killing beautiful Shire Horses and where the hell were the people who were supposed to be looking after them? In the years that followed, dead animals would be seen in their hundreds, but nothing affected me like the dreadful killing of those beautiful horses.

The defence of Arras should have been British left, French right. However we never did make contact with each other. After some three days of actively fighting of enemy aircraft and light mechanised infantry, we were astounded to hear on the BBC Radio that Arras had fallen, to be corrected the next day by an announcement Arras had been retaken by the French Army. We apparently did not exist. Neither did the French.

Eventually orders were given to move, march out in darkness, meet up with transport, move to new positions. Fog, blocked roads, inadequate maps, eventually led us out of the town, and into the countryside, but not before, in darkness, we were waved through a crossroads by a German Dispatch Rider. Obviously they were using some captured British transport.

News that our platoon of Bren Gun carriers had been almost wiped out, covering our retreat from Arras, came as a shock. These little lightly armoured track vehicles had swarmed in circles around a troop of enemy tanks, only to be picked off one by one, but gaining enough time for our convoy to escape. Their Captain Commander was posthumously awarded the V C and several others were also honoured.

After that it all became a case of dig in, hold this canal or that crossroads, always supposedly to the last man; last round. The orders always kept changing, sometimes before we had time to dig in; advance, retreat, advance, we lost all sense of time and direction. Officers missing, cut off when attending 'O' Group. Make for Dunkirk, at last a firm decision as to which way to go.

More dive bombing and machine gunning: dive into ditch, taking my Cup and Saucer Tree with me, wait for it to pass, then up and press on.

Standing on the brow of a hill, I could see the road stretching out in a large curve in front, so full of people it looked like a long caterpillar wriggling along. Decided to cut across country, thus it might be possible to cut off ten or twelve miles. Towards dark we came to a farmhouse, apparently empty, a few scrawny chickens running round, otherwise no movement. We had not eaten for about 48 hours, neither had we slept. Decided to scrounge something to eat and organise some rest. Two chickens quickly dispatched and in a pot of boiling water, potatoes were found, heaven; chicken and chips, decided to stay the night.

Chickens boiled, or at least parboiled, pile of chips all ready, then a cry of 'tanks'. Hells bells, a troop of some six tanks, all edging forward! Grab your equipment, get the hell out of here, chicken crammed into jacket, out the back, through the apple orchard, stop, check the platoon, one missing, then up he comes running and grinning. 'Where the hell you been? I stopped for the other chicken, I hope those Jerries are hungry, I've pissed on the chips.' Shared out the chickens, pressed on, resting and marching all night, next morning are caught up with the road and incredibly most of the Battalion, all fully equipped, dog tired, but still a coherent force.

10. APPROACH TO DUNKIRK

Suddenly the roads became blocked with transport of all kinds, the sides of the road were chock-a-block with vehicles which had been smashed, petrol tanks holed, tyres sliced open, engines smashed and wiring torn out. Occasionally we searched among the trucks for food, one or two were lucky with the odd tin of sardines or Bully Beef. Most of us were unlucky.

Looking back you could see the dark clouds of smoke from petrol and ammunition dumps, even supply dumps, blown up or set on fire. The sides of the road were saturated with petrol seeping from holed petrol tanks, the smell of petrol even blocked out the smell of burning. Some lucky chaps who had cigarettes were smoking, oblivious to the danger and too tired to care. It was like some nightmare from Dante's Inferno. Another defensive position, then relieved, separated once more from the Battalion, then the coast, the dunes and the beaches. Dunkirk burning to the left, and behind us ships around the quay, listing, smashed and burning. Troops sheltering in the sand dunes, waiting to be called off, bombed and strafed almost continuously by enemy aircraft. Small arms fire, even our friend the Bren Gun seemed totally inadequate. The question 'where the hell is the RAF?' was continuously asked, we were not to know that they also had suffered severe casualties.

Suddenly, incredibly, the sound of singing. 'She was only a bird in a gilded cage,' one of our favourite Company songs. We were reunited, dog tired, hungry, but happy to be a unit again. One quickly learned not to ask after individuals, just wait and hope. People were turning up all the time. Sleep, and safety in my Cup and Saucer Tree haven.

We formed a long line into the sea, the front of the line taken off. Then, about turn, march out again, discipline still as strong as ever Getting dark, another air raid, men running for some safety in the sand dunes, some kneeling and firing their rifles at the attacking planes. Near the shore line the whole scene turned into one of incredible destruction and magnificent beauty. Every time a footstep, bursting shell or flying bullet hit the sand it turned into a shower of fluorescent colours, a strange beautiful setting of a scene of incredible destruction, the burning town, and sunken ships in the sea, forming the most striking back drop. In the midst of all this someone shouting 'Get down you stupid sod.' I turned around and as he recognised me, he quickly apologised, 'Sorry Sergeant, didn't know it was you.' 'That's all right son.' Son! He was at least four or five years older than me, but how could I possibly tell him, a 6ft 6in Guardsman, tough as they come, that I was safe and secure having climbed up into the Cup and Saucer Tree of my childhood. Guardsmen were perfectly happy with their Colonels and Generals being bonkers, but they would become extremely unhappy with the idea of NCO's also being included in that category, especially one who had gained rapid promotion.

'Welsh Guards over here,' fall in, march out into the sea, chest high, almost swimming. The shorter ones were actually treading water. Clamber into a boat, ferried out to what looked like a cruiser, hell of a climb up rope ladders, with full equipment, carrying a rifle. Settle down in a metal corridor, about 2" of water sloshing about, the damn thing must be leaking! Almost asleep, this voice saying 'Give us your clothes Taff, I'll dry em on me boiler.' A cheerful Londoner (they get everywhere, we've even got a few in the Welsh Guards). Naked, curl up, my equipment and rifle across my knees, climb into my tree and fall fast asleep. Shaken awake, seeing someone in a strange uniform bending over me. I grabbed for my rifle, then that London voice again, 'Steady on Taff, I've brought your clothes back, sorry they ain't pressed. Here's your grub, it's all I could muster.' Sailor, you are a true blue hero. A mug of tea, well sugared and a slice of bread and jam, my first food in over three days.

Quickly enjoying my breakfast and dressing at the same time, it became apparent that we were docking, Dover I think. filing down the gang plank, photographers taking pictures, all a bit confusing.

11. DUNKIRK DISASTER

Beat the drum louder, pipe the pipes faster,
That is the way to drown out disaster.

The soldiers all huddled on sand dunes.
They had been fighting for days, without sleep.
They marched and they fought, in retreat and advance,
To end up on a beach and wait for a boat,
Shot up, bombed, and worse, with nothing to eat.

Long lines of soldiers leading into the sea.
Others lay face down, in the incoming surf,
They had paid the price of a soldier in war.
Some lay on stretchers, their minds past caring,
Orderlies and Doctors had done their best.

The backdrop of smoke from the township burning,
The dark silhouettes on the smashed up jetty,
Boats on their sides with their sterns in the air
Exploding and smoking, crews swimming free,
Struggling and screaming from their burns and wounds.
The diving planes screamed in, each in its turn,
Adding still more to the death and destruction.

Then, in the night, the sound of men singing,
A group of Welsh Guardsmen in dry throated harmony,
Soon to be joined by others, to voice their defiance.
And down on the shore, flashing and sparkling,
The fluorescent sand shone in all its brilliance.
Then the boats came in and took off some more.

The kind-hearted people met those who returned
With tea and cakes and cigarette rations;
They welcomed us with smiling kindness,
No-one would have guessed at their soldiers' plight
For this was the Army's greatest retreat.

The masters in Whitehall, masters still,
Their mistakes and blunders merely bad luck?
So Generals get Knighthoods, Politicians get votes,
A medal for the soldiers for the hell of Dunkirk.

Beat the drum louder, pipe the pipes faster,
That is the way they covered up disaster.

12. DISILLUSIONMENT IN ENGLAND

A Corporal Red Cap on the quay shouting 'dump your rifles here.' The crazy so and so, had everyone gone mad, we had clung to our arms through thick and thin, only to be ordered to dump them. Anyway, how the heck could we carry on fighting without rifles? I walked up, and told him in no uncertain terms that my platoon would not be dumping anything. If he wanted them, he was perfectly at liberty to come over and take them. Platoon fallen in, a nervous young line Regiment Officer approached and said 'You'll have to leave your weapons, Sergeant.' I saluted and, keeping control of myself, said 'Only on the direct order from one of our own officers, Sir.' By this time I was convinced that some dark plot was developing to hand over the whole of the British Army.

Then out of the blue, a Welsh Guard Captain, a kindly old gentleman from the last war, said 'Sorry men you will have to comply. Don't ask me why. I am as much in the dark as you.' Cocky bloody Red Cap. 'Rifles over her.' Order complied with, before he knew it he was up to his knees in rifles, the machine guns bouncing off his shiny shoes. One Guardsman, opening his ammunition pouch, produced a grenade and tossed it over to the Red Cap, saying 'You better have this as well, don't pull the pin, it is primed.' We never heard another shout from him.

Marching off, I could not help thinking that the worthies at Whitehall and the War Office had not only sold the Army short, they were now afraid of what the remains of that Army would do, hence the disarmament! Did they think that we would become a rabble and commit some mutinous action? So they were aware of their shortcomings!

After being pushed around from pillar to post, the Army decided that the easiest way to deal with the situation was to give us all travel warrants and send everyone on leave.

That seemed a satisfactory fudge to me, even though a deep feeling of guilt and anger would remain with me.

The slow train journey back to Wales seemed even longer that first trip back after Dunkirk. What would people say? How would they look at me? A professional soldier, kicked out of France, and now the whole country facing defeat!

Walking up Bridge Street, many people called out greetings and well wishes. Then it happened; the schoolmaster appeared, hand outstretched, gushing out praise and salutations. What had happened? Wasn't I the same person! the one to be ashamed of wanting to be a drunken, fornicating mercenary? I make no excuse for what I told him to do, ignoring his outstretched hand. In later years I would come to feel sorry for such short sighted behaviour, then frustration and anger took over.

Everyone was kindness itself. The old butcher neglecting a customer (that was really something) shouting 'I knew you were alright, saw your picture coming down the gang plank. Thought you were wounded, jacket stained in blood.' He was right of course, the

London sailor had dried my clothes, blood had clotted on the shoulder and front. It was the blood of a fellow sergeant who had been shot through the mouth, later to be honoured for bravery, in another war zone in Italy.

Although relaxing at home in Wales, a strong feeling of guilt, frustration and sometimes anger still persisted. The papers, and radio still insisted on glossing over the disaster of Dunkirk. Yes, it was a great achievement, soldiers and sailors had carried out acts of great heroism, and a very large number had been killed, wounded and taken prisoner, but it was not a victory.

Throughout history there are many instances of this habit we have of turning the shortcomings of people in command into victorious heroism, starting with the Charge of the Light Brigade and ending with Arnhem.

Even now, after this experience, there was no sense of urgency, nothing being done, the whole country appeared to be asleep. Did they not know that we faced absolute defeat like France and the rest of Europe? When would the fight back begin?

Having a rash on my chest caused by the salt water, I sought the help of my local doctor. A kindly person who tried to show his regard for me, by saying that if I would like a few more days at home he would willingly give me the necessary certificate! My frustration boiled up and spilled over. To my way of thinking this was exactly the problem with the British people. Everything was easy, no urgency, nothing mattered. Oh, I do hope he understood my reaction, after all he was only being kind and considerate. Two weeks complete rest, then the order to return.

Back to camp, new billets, three large houses on the west side of Wimbledon Common. Task: the defence of London and Home Counties. The Battalion was now more or less complete, headquarters in a block of flats in Putney. A visit by the King and a pep talk started the long hard climb back to normality.

13. WIMBLEDON - GAME, SET AND MATCH

Marching, swaggering, at the head of his troops,
Arms swinging, rifles gleaming, in perfect stride.
The people were all smiling, waving, some even crying,
For they all knew that we were back from Dunkirk;
Now to rest, re-train on Wimbledon Common.

The assistants of that posh hairdressing salon,
Leaned out of the windows on the first floor.
They waved and smiled like everyone else -
So many faces, intermingled in one vision.

Then I saw her, that beautiful face standing out;
Encircled by luscious, shining auburn hair.
A goddess right there, on Wimbledon High Street;
I knew I was possessed by that lovely creature.

Searching in vain each time I was free,
Waiting, spying, trying in any way to meet her.
Then one day on Guard Duty I saw her -
Cycling along, head in the air, enjoying her ride,
That beautiful hair out-shining the sun.

This vision came slowly towards me,
So I stepped out, demanded she stop.
She was startled and furious that
A soldier should accost a civilian.
Taken aback, I thought I had blown it.

Quickly rethinking my unsubtle approach,
I smiled and explained that I thought I knew her,
Having seen her looking down from above the shop.
But I now knew that I was mistaken -
That other person did not possess her beauty.

So please could I make up for a silly mistake?
And escort her to tea, coffee, cinema, anything!
She stared at me harshly 'What a damn cheek!'
Looking over her shoulder as she cycled away,
She smiled and said 'I'm free tomorrow, I leave the shop at one.'
So I went back on Guard Duty, another job well done.

14. MARRIAGE AND START OF A FAMILY

One day, returning from a route march along Wimbledon High Street, I noticed a very large expensive Ladies' lhairdressers shop, and in the windows above the shop the assistants leaning out and waving. One had the most beautiful auburn hair, and I said to myself 'That is someone I must meet.' We were married in April 1941.

Our first date was quite an eventful evening. We had arranged to meet on the corner of the west side of Wimbledon Common. An air raid had started, anti-aircraft guns were keeping up a steady barrage. This meant that shrapnel was falling like rain. As we walked toward each other, each keeping as close as possible to a very high garden wall, the whistling of a shell made itself heard and appeared to be making straight for us. We should of course have dived for shelter. I was too intent on making a good impression to even put on my steel helmet, and she, bless her, said afterward 'I certainly wasn't going to make a fool of myself, falling at his feet on our first meeting.' I found the shell the next morning, an unexploded one from some distant gun. It had hit the road and skidded off onto the common at a point midway between us.

My son, Richard, was born on the 18th February 1943. I of course was on some training exercise on Salisbury Plain.

He was a week old before I received the news.

One such exercise brought me a big problem. I had been instructed to lead the Divisional 'B' Echelon, several hundred vehicles of supplies, including all the cooks and food. Map reading was always my weak point, and on this occasion I excelled myself. After a couple of hours travelling across Salisbury Plain at night, I spotted just ahead of me a vehicle bearing the Divisional sign. Thinking I had caught up with Divisional 'A' Echelon, I promptly requested my driver to 'follow that lorry.' When dawn lit the sky, all was revealed. I had caught up with the tail of my own convoy which was going round in an enormous circle, like a scene from a cowboy western getting ready for an Indian attack.

Month after month, training in almost every part of the country, new equipment, new arms, such a lot to learn. We were now part of the newly formed Guards Armoured Division with the divisional sign of the ever open eye, a very distinctive sign, and despite the horrific air raids, a new feeling of confidence prevailed.

15. WORKING HIS TICKET

The amusing story of a Guardsman who beat the system and convinced the shrinks he was unfit for military service.

The talk in the Nissan Hut turned, as always, from sex to the absolute bloody awful life of the British Soldier, and then inevitably to the schemes for 'working your ticket', i.e. being thrown out as unfit for duty. Schemes like holding the little finger of the right hand just over the barrel of a 2" mortar and getting it blown off were discussed and discarded, the impact might blow the lot off, and in any case, the loss of a little finger was considered too trivial, there were many cases of soldiers with three fingers. Threatening the Sergeant Major with a bayonet, and many similar enterprises were all discarded. Surprisingly all this talk did no harm at all to the general moral and discipline. Quite the opposite in fact, it kept the dream alive to beat the system, now that would be something!

After some weeks of discussion one Guardsman stood up, looked around with a disdainful look and stated 'You bastards are too full of shite to even attempt it, but I will in the space of six months, obtain my full and final discharge.'

This statement quelled the usual banter of the hut, now here was something new, in just six months they would be minus one comrade! How the hell did this idiot propose to carry it out? He simply smiled and lightly tapped his forehead with his forefinger. What could he mean? Was he going to prove himself a loony, or did he mean he had the brains to carry out his plan?

Lights out at ten o'clock, at twelve precisely there was an ear splitting scream. Followed by all kinds of noises, the sound of a rifle having the bayonet stuck on. Suddenly the lights went on and the duty Sergeant Was shouting. The Guardsman ferociously stabbing his bayonet into his palliasse, shouting 'I've got the sod.' 'What do you think you are doing?' The Duty Sergeant was as perplexed as every one else. 'Hitler, Sergeant, he tried to get me, but I was too sharp for him.' 'You've been dreaming you silly bugger, take that bayonet off and get back to bed and put these lights out. I'll sort you out in the morning,' the Sergeant snorted in disgust. The Guardsman quietly murmured 'Round one to me I think.'

Next morning the Guardsman began what was to become almost a daily routine, being called up in front of his Company Commander for causing a disturbance, his case was dismissed just dreaming, they said.

Then the rumours started, his barrack room friends did the spreading of them - walking about in his sleep, looking for his long dead granny, walking and talking to his non-existent dog. Then he started in earnest. Whilst queuing up for his food on exercise, and being given a large tin of pilchards, (one tin between three men,) he started talking to his tin. 'Poor little fishy, who put you in there then? Did it hurt? Never mind, I'll soon have you out. What's your name fishy! Don't worry I won't bite you very hard.' All this within earshot of the Battalion Commander, who was at first speechless, staring goggle eyed at this idiot with a tin of pilchards. 'What is that?' he demanded. 'Get him out of sight before the Brigadier sees him!'

The Guardsman was led away and hidden behind a lorry , where his pals noticed him raise his forefinger and chalk an invisible mark in the air.

The next morning the Guardsman appeared before the Battalion Commander who ordered a medical report. The M O thought he was a little eccentric, an eccentric Guardsman - impossible! Only Officers were allowed to be eccentric, and a lot of them were!

After due consideration it was decided to transfer the Guardsman to headquarters, there the M O would be able to keep a closer watch over him. His duties would be simple, he could be a runner taking messages from one Company to another, and to make it easier he would have an army bicycle. Then the fun started. When sent on a message, he would hold the envelope in his mouth, grasp the handlebars with one hand, reach down with the other and pedal the bicycle with it, at the same time running alongside it. The excitement this caused as he raced through the small Somerset town had to be seen to be believed. People stopped and stared, shop keepers stood in their shop doorways, no doubt wondering what these idiots would be doing next, and what if the invasion started?

This was the final straw. He was sent off to the psychiatric hospital for a report. It is not known what he did there, but he must have done something because just two months later he was back.

The following morning, whilst I was waiting to be called in front of the Colonel to be reprimanded for some misdemeanour, the Guardsman emerged from seeing the Colonel. He had been given a complete and honourable discharge. I will always remember the wink he gave as he passed me. Two months later he was giving all Welsh Guards free rides on his Swansea tram. He had beaten the system, but was still in uniform as a Tram Conductor. Good luck, sunshine.

16. ACTION AT LAST

At last we were fully trained and mechanised, tanks, transports of every kind poured in. We were all geared up and raring to go; and with the new aeroplanes, fighters, bombers and gliders, we could now face our enemy on at least equal terms.

Eventually the great day arrived, and after what seemed like eternity on board ship, we landed in Normandy. What a sight, the sea seemed to be covered in ships of every kind, the air full of patrolling aircraft, all RAF. Vehicles and soldiers, stores of every description pouring into that small area of a bridgehead. What a contrast to Dunkirk. Now we could at last claim to be a professional army.

Disgorged from a landing craft and creeping softly through the surf, disaster, the damn truck conked out. We had been warned that if this happened, the self-starter button must not be used. Nothing for it other than jumping out, and swinging the starting handle. The advice was good and the truck easily started. I remember thinking that we were, in a way, fortunate to be an armoured Division: not for us that first blood-chilling dash up the beach. Our task was to push forward and break out of the enclosed area.

The small fields of the Bocage country proved extremely difficult for tanks, it seemed a long time before the final breakout. Then one night, dug in and waiting for orders just outside Caen, the barrage started. This was our first experience of such a really heavy shelling. Hundreds of artillery shells screaming overhead continuously for hours. The noise was so great it was impossible to hold a conversation. Nothing for it but head down, curled up in my slit trench, safe in my Cup and Saucer Tree, and soon asleep.

Awakened at dawn by the cessation of shelling, which had continued all night, the silence could almost be touched. Then the steady ominous drone of aeroplanes, bombers, hundreds of them, as wave after wave passed overhead. Then the crunch of bombs as they relieved themselves of their loads.

So this was what Montgomery had meant when he said 'I'll move when I am ready.'

The advance was slow, the roads and villages completely demolished, hampering movement, and incredibly German soldiers crept out of the rubble, still full of fight and using their machine guns, and anti-tank weapons to good effect. Eventually the objectives were reached and that particular battle won.

I was often asked after that episode how was it that I could sleep peacefully in the middle of all that noise going on, and as usual I could not tell them that I had climbed up into my Cup and Saucer Tree. This would only confirm what they already probably thought; h e is bloody mad, you know.

After several battles and skirmishes, slowly advancing, Calvados Country was slightly more open, but proved to be very difficult, finishing with the Battle for the Village of Montchamp, where already suffering from lack of reinforcements, we were to lose many more officers and men.

The attack proceeded, we went in without the tanks which were held up by blocked roads, and even before reaching the start line heavy casualties occurred. Again artillery was asked for and again refused. After some heavy fighting the centre of the village was reached. The enemy appeared to be withdrawing, a strategic move, as a massive counter attack came back, supported by tanks, cutting the Company in two. A withdrawal was ordered and completed with great difficulty. Casualties that day in the Prince of Wales Company were 37 men and officers killed or wounded. The rest of the Battalion suffered in a similar fashion. In just one week's fighting we had lost more than half of our Company.

17. BROTHERS

In the middle of a 'brew', reinforcements arrive.
Just twelve young men, we expected more,
For casualties had been many that day.
They drank their tea, looked around, and smoked.
All so young - just boys - tomorrow men!

Reading their names on the movement list,
I searched for the one I hoped had not come.
Then I saw him, no need to ask his name.
The likeness so marked, they had to be brothers.
The one now dead, unable to greet the other.

As I searched for words with which to tell him,
I thought of the mother in Wales, not yet grieving,
For she could not yet know of her elder son's death.
Probably thinking with pride of her sons together,
Each taking care, and looking after the other.

I had crept down the hedge, carried him back,
His killers now too lay dead, where he died.
And now I must tell his young brother all!
The boy who came to be with his brother,
And in just a few minutes would grow into a man!

18. ARMY DROPPING FROM THE SKY

Reinforcements came two days later, but not to full strength. One of the reinforcements was a young Guardsman who had been called up, done his training, and then at the request of his brother, a sergeant in my Company, posted to us. On arrival he had to be informed that forty eight hours previously his brother had been killed. I do hope I handled the situation with some delicacy.

There are few instances that NCO's cannot be trained for, this incident was one, another is fortunately even more rare, but much more difficult, and does sometimes occur in even the most highly disciplined troops. This is when a soldier, completely exhausted, shaking with nerves, holding his hands over his ears to drown out the scream of shells, begs to be removed from the situation. What do you do? Make him stay and try to get over it? Send him back to casualty? Either way, whatever the decision, the risk is the same. His life will probably be ruined for years to come, you can only rely on your intuition.

Although Victory seemed now to be within our grasp, nothing could stop us, but many more battles had to be fought, victories and some tragic setbacks had to be overcome.

One of the setbacks was the battle of Arnhem. We were unable to reach the town and bring relief to the troops parachuted in. Doomed from the start. This was one of those battles which produced incredible acts of bravery against impossible odds, but which should never have occurred at all. Market Garden, as the plan was called, was in itself a very ambitious plan and had it worked, would have been one of the great victories of history. The organisation, the logistics of the whole scheme were enormous, almost as great as the invasion itself, but with a fraction of the time available to carry it out.

The first part of Market Garden worked quite well, bridges were secured, and troops roared through. The method employed was simple and involved airborne troops being dropped, straddling the bridges. The ground forces then forcing a path through the enemy to link up with the airborne troops. Only one bridge caused delay. It had been blown, the Bailey Bridge was eventually installed and the attack continued.

Nimegan Bridge caused all sorts of problems, it was partly blown, there was a gaping hole on one side, this did not prevent tanks and heavy vehicles crossing. The area over the bridge between Nimegan and Arhham was nicknamed the 'Island' and was a horrible place to be in. Digging in was impossible, each time an inch was dug out it filled up with water. The one road which stood up above the surrounding fields soon became littered with burned out vehicles. As soon as one tried to pass anything, you were immediately bogged down. The whole area appeared to be flooded, we were destined not to reach Arnham.

It is a strange and unforgettable sight to see an army dropping from the sky, dangling from parachutes, or skimming down in gliders, the swish of their flight was such a contrast to the gentle waving parachutes, and of course, as this was war the inevitable sight of some being blown up , or crash landing in flames.

19. TASTE OF DEATH

Whilst advancing through Holland, having reached our objective for that day, we settled down for the night in a farmyard. Everyone dug in, or selected safe spots for sleep. I decided to sleep in a space between a high wall and what I thought was a vegetable clamp of potatoes or turnips, a mound of earth about five foot high and rounded on the top.

Having finally eaten, and done all my duties, I settled down for a few hours' sleep. I was just wrapped in a blanket, with another for a pillow, feeling quite safe from any stray shells should the enemy start being aggressive.

At 'Stand To', one hour before dawn, I was conscious of having a splitting headache, and the most disgusting taste in my throat and mouth. All I could do was wait for 'Stand Down', when I could grab a mug of tea and, if lucky, a quick wash and cleaning of teeth.

As the daylight gradually lightened my surroundings, things began to take shape and I could see part of a body sticking out of the 'vegetable clamp.' It finally turned out to be a mass grave, hastily covered up.

I drank two tots of Army ration rum, neat, and still the 'taste of death' remained in my throat.

Whenever I hear someone talk of the smell of death, I always think, 'surely they mean the taste of death?' and I reach for an extra strong mint, or a shot of Scotch! The taste remains, not nearly so strong, but it's still there.

20. ROAD TO VICTORY

The period 29th August to 3rd September involved an advance of 360 miles from Conde-Sur-Nireau to the centre of Brussels. This included, amongst other towns and villages, the City of Arras, the area we had defended in the period before Dunkirk. As always the people came out in droves, waving, cheering, showering us with fruit and flowers. Our Company Commander, Major J M Miller, D S O., M C (later to become Colonel Sir John Miller D S O., M C., Equerry to the Queen) was able to visit our old billets in the village of St Nicholas, and collected most of his kit, which he left behind in the hurried retreat to Dunkirk. He was given a tremendous reception by the villagers, all asking for news of various members of the Company. A welcome interlude in a trying time.

On the 3rd September we were teamed up with our 2nd Battalion, a tank battalion, this was to be the first time both Battalions had been put together as a fighting force.

The Commander of the 30th Corp, of which we were part, had devised a simple, straight forward plan, seize and capture Brussels, Welsh Guards Group route 'A', Grenadier Guards Group Route 'B' Brussels 100 miles ahead, last one in is a sissy, or words to that effect.

The starting gate was to be opened at 0600 hours, and we were off. Skirting round Donai proved difficult, but by 0930 hours we were bursting over the Franco/Belgian border. The cheering crowds in France were terrific, however the reception in Belgium exceeded even that, flowers and cheers all the way.

The route went through Antoiny, Louje, Ath, and Eingheim, we sailed through all opposition. When the lead tanks got held up, we debussed, dealt with the problem, back on the trucks, then pushing on, cutting through the enemy, now in full flight. Tanks flat out at speeds of 40 miles an hour. Ignoring all casualties and prisoners, these were left for others to deal with, usually the ever present patriots.

At Eingham we caught up with a fleeing Enemy Division, many vehicles, and some horse drawn transport were scattered in all directions, and for some miles the road was littered with abandoned and blazing vehicles. The patriots had a busy time rounding up all the prisoners. One could not help thinking of those days four years earlier, when our position was much the same as that of the fleeing Germans. The civilians, in their hunger for meat, quickly hacked huge steaks from the dead horses, to provide themselves with a feast.

We occasionally came into villages where the patriots had already taken over, there were sorry scenes of groups of women, holding other terrified women, having their hair clipped off in chunks, sometimes skin and all, whilst their houses were being ransacked, furniture thrown into the street, and in one instance a broom being pushed through the roof from the room below, trying to destroy it completely. These were the women who had openly cohabited with German soldiers. It was pitiful to see, but beyond our control.

Our orders were to get to and hold three strong points in the city, and that evening No 1 Squadron 2nd Batt Welsh Guards (Tanks) and Prince of Wales Company 1st Batt Welsh Guards (Infantry) became the first troops to enter and liberate the City of Brussels.

The reception was beyond belief, the whole population seemed to be on the streets, it was impossible to move except at a snail's pace, our trucks and tanks were covered in civilians and flowers, one driver received a black eye when a bottle of wine was tossed into his cab by a delirious well wisher. He grumbled half-heartedly 'Come all this bloody way, without a problem, and a civvy does me in with a bottle of wine.' All this happening with enemy machine gun fire whipping down side streets, half track vehicles scurrying away, shooting to clear a path.

Everything was chaotic, we were either mobbed by civilians or shot at by Germans.

I got lost, but then I was in good company, so did the Company Commander, but with the help of eager civilian guides, we both caught up with the company in what, I think, was called the 'Cinquante Nairo', a magnificent square with three Triumphant Arches. Crowds stayed with us all night, sleep was impossible, but for once I did not need the comfort of the Cup and Saucer Tree.

The following morning we were to move out of the City and continue our advance. The Company Commander decided we would do it in style, we formed up as though going on a Guard Mounting at Buckingham Palace and marched to attention, arms swinging in perfect order, and marched out of the City to be picked up later by our transport. The populace loved it, they sang, danced, marched alongside, the whole place exploded with cheering happy people.

The Guards Armoured Division, led by the Welsh Guards, had the satisfaction of making not only Regimental history, but world-wide history. We had covered 360 miles in six days. On the sixth day we had covered 100 miles, which is by far the longest advance ever made by an armoured division in one day, not even surpassed in Russia.

An experience never to be forgotten. And that is the reason why on 3rd September visitors are often surprised by, and not aware why, the famous monument of the 'Manikin Pis' is dressed up in full dress uniform of the Welsh guards, Busby and all, in remembrance of that day so long ago that the Welsh Guards liberated their City.

21. THE LAST BATTLE

In the first weeks of March, commencing on the 8th day, the guards Armoured Division were heavily engaged in the area of Bonninghardt and Wesel in the Rhineland. The first Battalion Welsh Guards, with the Second Battalion tanks were still together as a fighting unit, although by this time a company of Scots Guards made up for previous casualties.

In Bonninghardt itself there was a great deal of hand to hand fighting. It is in such situations that soldiers are brought sharply face to face with war, you actually see, and touch your enemy, and are not shooting at some advancing or retreating figure.

As other Divisions were gradually closing in on Wesel, the Division was relieved, and, although we were not aware of it at the time, the First Battalion Welsh Guards had fought their last battle. We were no longer to wear that distinctive shoulder flash, of which we were so proud, the 'Ever open Eye'.

We went back to a rest centre we had used before, just outside Nimegan, in a school, part of which had become a hospital, next to a convent. The nuns were always cheerful, as in our previous visits, we tried to help them as much as possible.

Our first visit was at the time of the battle for Arnham, we were withdrawn from Nimegen Bridge, and the 'Island' for a few days rest,. My company were billeted in the old school. Two of the classrooms were turned into a hospital ward for the local people.

It was manned by the local doctor, assisted by two trained nurses. One of the nurses on that first day came to me and shyly asked if I could spare the time to visit, as her charges had not yet had the pleasure of seeing a British Tommie. She explained that one of her charges, a young man, had studiously been learning English, keeping his text book under his pillow, regardless of frequent visits by German inspectors.

Of course, I jumped at the chance to speak to that young boy who had studied English for almost two years, but had never actually used the spoken word, it was a very great privilege. The words simply tumbled out, sometimes in beautiful classic phrases, and sometimes completely out of context, after that first day I spent many happy hours in that ward, after all this time I can still hear his eager voice 'Please David, if I bend my head, I bow, and I reach to a tree, I still hold a bow, no matter the spelling.'

The elderly people in the ward were so pleased, many were in tears. One old lady held my hand, she had long since given up hope of ever seeing her country free, but now there was a fresh gleam in her eye, she could now fight on.

Armed with a few bars of chocolate and two bottles of champagne repatriated from a German food dump. I paid another visit. They all enjoyed a sip or two of champagne, and a square of chocolate. I was worried that this would interfere with their medication and said as much to the nurse, who simply replied 'But this is their only medication.' I kept a regular supply of tins of soup, bully beef, etc. going for as long as I could.

The nuns too were very kind and we tried to help them Their monastery was next door to the school-hospital. I managed to get the company cobbler, busy repairing as many of their shoes as he could. He was deeply touched one day when a nun he was working with came up with an egg in her hand and insisted he accept it. She had waited weeks for this little luxury to be allocated to her, she obviously needed its nourishment, it was probably her only possession, yet she was giving. it away. He turned the tables by saying that the egg really didn't matter to him, but if she so wanted to show her appreciation of what he was doing, then could she please get Mother Superior to bless the silver cross given to him by his wife. The effect was as expected, the convent all said prayers over the cross and were so happy to do so.

One other incident at this time was very amusing. I was standing on the side of the road when a Divisional Staff car approached at speed. The Divisional Commander was on his way to the front line. I stood to attention, and gave my smartest salute, then a voice shouted, 'Hello Bert, how you doing?' I caught a glimpse of a cheeky face grinning at me, and the General looking out of the rear window, smiling broadly. Bert! I had not been called that since my school days, for years everyone called me David! And how dare that blasted driver and his General take the mickey out of a Warrant Officer in the Brigade of Guards. Some years after the war ended, I learned the truth about that mysterious episode. It was indeed someone from my old school, younger than me, so perhaps that was why I had not recognised him. He was a young man, John Breeze, who sadly was killed some weeks later. He had written home with great delight at the shock he had given me, this story was related to me by his father when he bought me a drink in the village pub. If only it could have been Johnnie buying me that drink! That would have been a story truly worth telling.

22. `FAREWELL TO THE REGIMENT

Whilst on a tour of Wales with the Company, I was given the instruction to proceed to Sandhurst as an instructor, I disliked the idea and tried desperately to stay with the Battalion. My Company Commander was also leaving, to command a training school in Warminster, I think he also tried to stay. He smiled as he usually did when faced with something his heart was not in.

I was proud and so pleased that on the day I left, he assembled the Company, thanked me for my support and presented me with a silver cigarette case suitably inscribed, one of my treasured possessions.

After a short spell at Sandhurst I managed to arrange my transfer to the Training Battalion at Sandown Park Racecourse, there was something reassuring about being billeted in a racing stables, I could lay on my bed day-dreaming of that other stable with the big Shire stallion once more sharing my life.

Despite pressure and offers of further promotion, I decided that life with my family came first. On the 21st April 1946 I returned to civilian life, having served in the Army for exactly eight years and 88 days, to commence the second part of my life plan.

It was of course much later than expected, and I was now a family man with a wife and son.

23. THE SOLDIER ARTIST

(For Rex Whistler)

I gazed at the beautiful murals of Plas Newydd,
Remembering the artist, the man that created
Those beautiful, vivid, bright scenes.
And then I recalled another such place
Equally vivid, in a much darker setting.

The small fields of the Bockage Country,
Its thick hedgerows concealing heavy guns,
Tanks on fire, their crews often burning,
Soldiers rushing, dodging and falling.

Then the sight of this talented man,
A Captain lying dead on the ground
Those creative hands now lifeless and still
Never again, never again to hold a brush!

24. NEVER LOOK BACK

Living in retirement has its compensations. We now have time to do what we like, when we like, where we like, without complications.

Whilst on our way back from a visit, I thought it would be nice to have a look at my old home, 'Waterlow Cottage'. Had it altered or changed in any way?

The pictures started to form in my mind. The old wooden bridge arched over the railway line, the smell of the smoke as the trains thundered underneath. The trains, I knew, were now extinct - Dr Beeching closed the line down. Still, it would be pleasant to see the old bridge.

Then the mind pictures simply tumbled out. The stream criss-crossing the old lane, two footbridges, perfect for Pooh Sticks. The trickling brook, which we frequently dammed to create a paddling pool. The old orchard with apples, plums, damsons and pears. We frequently went scrumping. No one seemed to worry.

In the adjoining field in the corner by the orchard, a large mound, which looked rather like a hill fort. It had a huge oak tree on its top, a perfect place to sit and survey the landscape, whilst enjoying a pocket full of purloined plums. The two horses that carried out the work of the farm usually shared the shade of the tree.

One day the old farmer came by as I was sitting under the tree. To my surprise, he sat down beside me. He had arthritic hips and was always in pain. We talked of his horses, and he explained why only one horse was allowed a foal each year. They took it in turns year by year, that way he always had one horse to shoulder most of the work whilst the other was with foal. In my teens I worked all one summer for this kindly old farmer.

Memories! Mind pictures! The old water meadow stretching out from the foot of the mound, ablaze with colour - cowslips, hair bells, wild white daisies, buttercups, all competing to brighten each day. The path that meandered through all this beauty, crossing the ditches on old wooden bridges, just trunks of trees with one side roughly hewn flat.

This meadow had not been cultivated, or enriched with anything other than the natural fertilising by the animals.

Always the flock of geese grazing, the old gander on guard. Boys in short trousers had to be quick. The old gander's serrated teeth hurt bare legs.

The scene was always the same, and probably had been for a century or more, a truly breathtaking, beautiful spot.

In the old gravel lane, the banks were always covered in primroses and violets, and the hedges with dog roses.

A gypsy caravan usually occupied the vacant little spaces on the sides of the lane, with its pot hanging on a tripod over the open fire. The men, as usual, making pegs which the gypsy ladies sold in the villages and towns. Another rural scene to be savoured in one's mind.

My mind was filled with anticipation as I drove up the lane. Then the truth was revealed. The wooden bridge was gone, the railway cutting underneath filled in and levelled off with the earth from the mound in the corner of the field. The two footbridges and the old brook no longer visible, the water was now piped underground. The orchard, too, had vanished - even the large walnut tree routed out.

A tarred road replaced the gravelled lane, and continued across the field, replacing the old path. The water meadow was now a landscaped caravan park, neatly arranged, in line abreast around a small lake, obviously done with a lot of care and thought. The timeless beauty of that old water meadow was now lost forever.

As I drove across the field on this hard road toward the old farm, I wondered 'what next?' Nothing could be more of a shock. Well it was! The old farm was built in the shape of a three sided square. The midden, always gently steaming, was in the middle. The pigs, cattle and horses each occupied a side. A small stream flowed past on the open side.

These buildings had vanished and, in their place, new brick executive holiday suites lavishly appointed.

I have every sympathy with farmers who have, these days, to diversify or die. However, this appeared to me to be not diversification, but annihilation.

The lesson I learned was never look back, your memories will be shattered. Always look ahead and plan for new memories to replace the old.

25. THE WATER MEADOW - A POEM FOR TWO VOICES - 1930 - 1998

Tail flicking wagtails, yellow and pied,
Darting, and catching their insect food,
Their young at their heels, begging for more.
Tail swishing cows cropping ancient herbage,
Their pollen covered hooves, and yellow lips.
Fertilising the masses of buttercups, and cowslips
By disturbing the insects who help in the act.

The old footpath is now a tarmac drive,
The stream unseen in an underground tunnel.
Lines of chalets all neatly conforming
With space in between for a shining four by four.
Mountain bikes, dogs on leads, drying towels,
Children happily running, shouting and playing,
Has anyone told them of nature's way?

The Farmer's wife's Christmas Geese busily eating,
All growing fat to command a good price.
The gander alert, and bossing his flock,
Head outstretched, hissing out warnings,
Then rushing to attack those not heeding,
Wings outstretched - half-flying - half-running
Into the fray like a ship at Trafalgar.

The sculptured pond, with its quota of ducks,
Grass neatly clipped by a ten-foot mower.
The tractor buzzes round, now the ditches are filled in,
All geared up to progress, whilst making money.
Everything done to please the residents,
I hope they are happy with their annual visit.
Do they realise that this is man's way, not nature's?

High in the sky a heavenly chorus as skylarks hover.
House martins, swallows, feed on the wing,
Ducking, swerving in scintillating flight.
Plovers and corncrakes, searching the ground
For beetles, ladybirds, and daddy long legs.
They feast, grow strong, as nature intended,
One species sustaining the life of another.

The old farm buildings have all disappeared.
Cow bays, pigsties, and sweet smelling stables
Now replaced with red-bricked executive suites.
No grunting old pig with pink squeaky piglets.
Just shiny big cars, and plump city men.
Loud music, senseless laughter, infantile jokes,
Replacing the sounds of animals, and nature at work.

The fauna stretching out in its infinite beauty,
Ragged robin, marsh marigold, and spiky mouse tail.
All growing together in jumbled harmony,
Their names competing with the beauty of species.
Meadowsweet, Pennyroyal, Cuckoo flower, Gentian,
cabbage thistle, Buttercups, Cowslips and Daisies,
Reflecting the centuries of nature maturing.

The Water Meadow now changed to a Holiday Village
They tried very hard to make everything fit in,
But now it is as man, and not nature intended,
A century of nature, lost forever, by human endeavour.

26. A GENTLE MAN

He is a country man, a quiet, simple man:
And more - he has seen the Red Kites at play,
High in the sky, whirling, diving in aerobatic flight.
And he has seen the Buzzards in courtship
In mid-air, almost colliding, they gently touched,
Never impeding their fast flight of joy.

He is a lucky man to have seen such things,
And more - he has stroked his lover's auburn hair;
He kissed her good-night in the blackout of war;
As real today as it was that first night.

He is a fortunate man to have wedded her,
And more - he has heard the cry of his first born,
Seen him grow up and marry his own lovely bride.
The growing up of his grandchildren brought him great joy,
The prospect of their children greater joy still.

He is an elderly man to have had all this!
And more - he has smelled wars, death and destruction,
Lived through it all, and smelled once again
The heather on the hills and the gorse by the river
Just as he did when he was a child.

He is a thankful man to have lived this life!
And more - he has tasted this life to the full,
Lived it as well as he knew how.
An elderly, simple, fortunate, country man;
A happy man - that's me!

EPILOGUE

Dark clouds scurrying across the sad sky,
Rushing together, to be darker still.
Bonded in blackness, to start a big storm.
A message of doom! Then, the rain drops fell.

Pulling off the road, I stopped the car,
Staring in horror at the place you should be,
Refusing to believe you were not there.
My beautiful Cup and Saucer Tree - gone.

Not troubled by cascades of cold lashing rain,
I stood \and looked at your mutilated stump
And then, in the field, the dark circle of ash -
All that was left of your funeral pyre.

What demented axeman had cut you down?
How, if not by a madman, could this be done?
Not for fuel to warm a family,
For there were fallen trees, and timber in plenty.

In despair, I stood in the storm -
Tears, raindrops. Raindrops, tears.
No matter which fell from nose to chin,
My guardian, my castle, my tower now at rest.

Why wasn't I there to guard or defend you?
To offer you succour, as you always offered me?
I was far away in a Continental war.
I should have know, I should have felt your distress.

They say you had some terrible disease.
Amputation the cure, the tree doctor said,
Not specifying which. Do trees contact cancer?
Whatever it was, I will not accept it!

For most of my life you were alive,
You were real - now only to me!
You were, you are, still in my mind,
And will remain there always until I die.